A Lincolnshire Chi...

on old pic

Bria

3. Bishop Norton. The children take a break from school to pose outside their classroom. Card from a Market Rasen publisher. The 1880 Education Act had made school attendance compulsory for all children aged five to ten, though Board Schools (run by a School Board rather than a church) locally could insist on attendance up to the age of 13.

**Designed and published by
Reflections of a Bygone Age,
Keyworth, Nottingham 2011**

**Printed by Adard Print & Typesetting
Services, The Green, Ruddington,
Nottingham**

£3.95

Introduction

Growing up in Lincolnshire in the early 20th century was a hugely different proposition to the lifestyle experienced by children today. With opportunities for travel restricted, life inevitably centred around the local community, where facilities for organised leisure would be limited. Parents had much less leisure time to spend with children and they often had to occupy themselves.

Picture postcards provide an amazing insight into a world where youngsters could feel much more secure in their environment, especially on the streets, where traffic posed a minimal hazard. Many of the cards in this book show wide streets untroubled by anything faster than a horse and cart, occupied by groups of children who were able to play in them safely.

Many postcards also show organised community events - fetes, processions and celebrations - where children were kitted out in their best clothes. Children were involved in these events either as participants or spectators, observing events, learning trades and skills, working and being an integral part of the community.

Of course, the faclities we today take for granted were not widely available, and local sports clubs often assimilated children into open-age teams when they were good enough, rather than sponsoring lots of different age-group teams.

Postcards were at the height of their popularity and usage from 1902-14, the decade or so before the First World War, and the unspoken poignant question hanging over every photographic card from this era featuring children is *" what was their fate in the war?"*. Edwardian Britain is largely looked on as a golden age, an idyllic period before a cataclysmic conflict, and while that image has flaws - it was also in some places a time of violent industrial unrest, political struggle, minimal household service provision and chronic poverty - the idea has a certain legitimacy, especially in Lincolnshire, with its profusion of peaceful villages and quiet market towns.

The vast majority of the postcards in this book were produced by local publishers, and come from the collection of the late John Wilson of Saxilby.

Picture postcards were first published in Britain in 1894, but it was not until a decade later that they began to take off, when in 1902 the Post Office allowed a message to be written on the address side. This meant that the whole of one side was available for the picture and obviously gave more scope to publishers. Photographic viewcards became very popular, and the postcard developed into the most important way of communicating news or messages, in much the same way as the telephone is used today. The years up to 1914 were the 'Golden Age' of picture postcards, when millions of imaginative designs covering every subject under the sun were published by a host of national, regional and local firms or individuals. These latter published postcards of streets, buildings and events locally, and have left us with an amazing pictorial record of the early 20th century. Many are featured in this book and, where known, the publisher of the card is included in the caption.

Brian Lund
July 2011

Front cover: Local children outside the church at Dunholme on a postcard c.1905 published by the 20th Century Photographic Co.

Back cover (top): The Maypole at Willingham Fete 1912 on a card published by Howard Welchman of Gainsborough.

(bottom) : Decorated float at Gainsborough. Card produced by Chas. W. Stephenson.

4. The Lincoln Typhoid outbreak of 1905 was a traumatic experience for everyone, and the children on this postcard look pretty serious - though it was not done to smile for the photographer in Edwardian days! This card shows the collection of fresh water 'supplied by T. Peel Esq' (a butcher near Newport Arch in the city). The card was posted at Lincoln on 7th August 1908. The epidemic, caused by contaminated water from the River Witham, peaked in January 1905. Over 1,000 cases were reported and 131 people died.

5. Children in pierrot costume celebrate Mayday at Colsterworth. Card published by G. Barker of Colsterworth and posted at Grantham in August 1909. *"These"*, explains the writer, *"are maypole plaiters in Easton Park at the Flower show"*.

6. A street scene in Horse Market, Caistor showing a horse-drawn cart and children playing outside. The absence of any other street traffic was commonplace in villages in the Edwardian period. This postcard was sent with Christmas greetings from the village to a Hampshire address in December 1905.

7. Children playing by the local stream at Castle Bytham, again untroubled by traffic. The card was actually posted in London to a Doncaster couple in October 1926, but was probably published some years earlier.

8. A typical scene in Caythorpe c.1912 outside the local post office, where the postmaster, doubling as the general store owner, is stood in his long white apron. As so often happened with postcard photos a century ago, the photographer has organised a group of local children to provide animation.

9. The children's festival parading through the streets of Colsterworth where the older girls wear a ring of flowers in their hair and the younger children wear bonnets. All the observers are wearing their 'Sunday best' with the gentlemen in waistcoats and suits and the ladies in their long-flowing skirts and hats. The card was posted at Grantham in August 1906.

10. Maypole dancing at Corby, with the boys dressed in white 'clown' costumes and the girls in pretty white dresses, with a few having coloured sashes around their waist. The card was posted out of season on Christmas Eve 1906 from Grantham to Great Yarmouth.

11. A decorated wagon at Crowland, full of children all trying hard to look at the camera. The card was posted at Peterborough in July 1908. Crowland, a market town in south Lincolnshire, had a population of just over 2,700 in 1904. At the confluence of the River Welland and the Catchwater Drain, it is most famous for its abbey.

12. Both the children and adults look ready for a hard day's work on Eastoft Road, Crowle, with their barrows and carts. Card posted at Crowle in April 1919. Crowle, in the north of the county, had a population of just over 2,700.

13. A photocall on the bridge over the stream at Dunholme. The majority of the girls are dressed in white pinafore dresses with large collars and wide brimmed hats, and the boys in flat caps. Dunholme, six miles north-east of Lincoln, was a small village of some 300 people in Edwardian days.

276. U.M. Sunday School Treat. Dunholme. 1912. J.S.&S.

C.R. OUTRAM
FAMILY BUTCHER

14. The outing for the United Methodists' Sunday School, a lovely treat for all on the horse-drawn carriages at Dunholme in 1912. Special days out for children organised by churches or businesses were a feature of Edwardian life. The postcard, published by J. Simonton & Son, was posted at Lincoln in July 1912.

15. A boy in his working apron pictured outside the butcher's shop at Eagle Moor, near Lincoln, with his dog and the local butcher, possibly his boss C.R. Outram. Children normally began working at the age of 12 when they left elementary school, unless they were one of the privileged who went to private schools.

16. The village post office - along with church and pub, one of the centres of a community in Edwardian England, was a popular spot for assembling locals for a photograph. This is Eastoft, a parish near Crowle with a 1904 population of 454.

17. The 1st XI hockey team at Lincoln Christ's Hospital Girls' High School in the 1912-13 season. Originally a 17th century charity school, LCHGHS emerged in 1893, based on Lindum Road, charging fees until 1944. The pupils here would be exposed to team games heavily as part of the school ethic. For children over 12 whose parents could not afford school fees, the best hope of organised sport was through a local church team.

18. A crowd is gathered at Epworth for the proclamation of George V in 1910. Communal celebrations for big events were as commonplace in Edwardian Britain as now. All generations are united and as you can see there are only a few gentleman not wearing a hat (mainly stood around the lovely street light).

EPWORTH MAY 19 1910

The children have been placed at the front of the picture and are also universally hatted! No photographer was credited on the postcard. Epworth, in the Isle of Axholme, boasted 1,856 souls in 1904.

19. Two little girls on their horse and cart, virtually identical with their matching outfits, hair in ringlets and a lovely little bow to finish off. The card was published by W.E. Phillips of Fulstow, almost certainly placing the location there.

20. A marvellous Edwardian street scene on Trinity Street, Gainsborough, with only sedately-paced delivery carts challenging a group of children for possession of the space. The card was posted at Gainsborough in March 1905, sent to Broadholme, near Saxilby, with the message *"Shall run over on Saturday afternoon"*.

21. Same street, different time. A postcard published by the Doncaster Rotophoto Co. and posted in February 1920 shows a new generation of children standing outside their local shop on Trinity Street, with the clothes that they are wearing looking like they have seen some 'rough and tumble'.

22. A street view at Gosberton. Five miles north-east of Spalding, Gosberton had a railway station on the Great Northern & Great Eastern Joint Railway line from March to Lincoln, and a population of 1,825 when Edward VII was crowned.

23. This must have been a fascinating time for the assembled youngsters, with various modes of transport outside Glentham Post Office. Two suited men sit proudly in their car.

24. Grantham's wide Westgate, with not a vehicle in sight and children happily strolling and chatting in the street. The girls are in pinafore dresses and the men in three-piece suits. Surprisingly for a postcard of a town, no photographer or publisher is credited. Posted from Grantham to the "Eagle Hotel" at Woodhall Spa in July 1906, the message reads: " *Dear Lucy, How is it I have not received your letter, hoping you are not ill*". Ah, the slow pace of personal communication in those days!

25. Grasby village in north Lincolnshire, where the local children are outside playing in their white pinafore dresses. The photographer would frequently enrol local children to add animation to pictures.

Visit of King & Queen to Grimsby. July 22nd 1912. Children Singing. 5. F.C.C.Series.

26. The vast crowd is full of schoolchildren singing in honour of the King and Queen's visit to Grimsby on July 22nd 1912. The Royal couple were in the area to open a new dock at Immingham. 'F.C.C. series' postcard.

GRIMSBY AND CLEETHORPES VOLUNTEER TRAINING CORPS.
INSPECTION AT PEOPLE'S PARK, MARCH 14TH, 1915. (3)

27. The military connection. Volunteer Training Corps at People's Park, Grimsby, in 1915. The band at the head of the procession is made up largely of young teenagers, while potential recruits made up of older lads - this dates before conscription - are marching behind. Card published by Porri's News Bureau, Grimsby.

1st Barrow B.P. Scouts.

28. The Barrow-on-Humber B.P. (Baden Powell) Scout troop c.1910 on a postcard published by B. Parker of Barton-on-Humber.

29. Itinerant photographers toured schools taking group pictures. This is Waddington Infant School, classes 1 & II, about 1910. The card was published by a firm from Worthing, Sussex, which would aim to sell multiple copies to every parent! The class teacher is on the back left. In 1902, funding of schools was entrusted to Local Education Authorities. Four miles south of Lincoln, Waddington had a 1904 population of 770.

High Street, Horncastle

30. This postcard of Horncastle High Street was published by George Washington Wilson, a top Scottish postcard firm. Today this is normally a very busy traffic junction.

31. Great Hale fete on a postcard by an uncredited photographer. A wagon to the left the crowd with even the bikes and their spokes being decorated with flowers and co village of Great Hale, five miles south-east of Sleaford, had 568 people living there in

GREAT HALE

...stcard is trimmed up with flowers and there are lots of floral bouquets within ...per. There are two gentlemen in the crowd wearing 'funny' face masks. The

32. The local Ingoldmells farrier at work is being observed by a farmer and his children on a cold winter's day. Postcard published by J. Simonton of Sheffield, and posted at Skegness in August 1913.

33. Empire Day at Spittlegate School, Grantham, on a postcard published by local photographer Emery. In 1918 education was made compulsory for all children up to the age of 14, and the Education Act of that year also made possible the creation of nurseries and special needs provision.

34. Party time in Louth, 1911. The children include members of the local Boys' Brigade.

35. Seaside entertainment for children was a feature of most beaches in Edwardian Britain. A large crowd has turned out on Mablethorpe beach for a performance by Clements' 'Royal Entertainers' (sands daily, Pavilion nightly). Even on a hot day, everyone is turned out in their Sunday best with full suits and flat caps. The postcard, published by Valentine of Dundee, was posted at Mablethorpe in September 1916.

S 5711 THE SANDS, MABLETHORPE

36. Many people are venturing into the sea at Mablethorpe, still wearing their clothes with just the odd sock removed so they can dip their toes. W.H. Smith & Son 'Kingsway' series postcard, sent to Bradford on 27th July 1914 - five days before the outbreak of war. *" Having a splendid time here it is a lovely place plenty of sands"*, wrote Edith to Doris.

37. Queen Street, Market Rasen. Two little girls with pigtails pose along with a few locals. Even town streets were safe places to walk and play. Card published by Starbuck.

38. Five boys and girls underneath the fancy oil light at Metheringham, not looking particularly happy. The boys with their flat caps on and the girls with their berets have been asked to pose by the local Navenby photographer, W. Odling, to add some life to the scene.

39. Medlam School at Carrington, seven miles north of Boston, and a group photo of the children, all looking very well presented. They vary in ages from the youngest on the left of the postcard to the older children and teachers to the right. The school was opened in 1881 and closed in 1987. Children from the village now attend school at Stickney. Postcard published by The Express Photo Co., Boston.

40. Catching crabs was and still is a popular activity on the Lincolnshire coast. *"Would you like to join the crab catchers. We are having a very nice time"*, wrote the sender of this postcard from Mablethorpe in 1920. Card published by Alfred J. Lougton of Southwell.

41. Bannerman Road in New Holland, a typical residential street scene from c.1910.

42. A group of children on Delph Bridge, North Hykeham, and by the stream bank, there is a child sleeping in the grass! Even the boys in the trees are dressed smartly with jackets and flat caps. Children were given much more freedom to play and explore compared with today's often claustrophobic parental restrictions on their movements.

43. A group of children in the street at North Scarle, with the unusually-named "Sedan Inn", at the end of the street. It later became known as "The Sedan Chair" until its closure in the late 1970s. It looks like winter time as all the children and parents are wrapped up warm in coats, scarves and thick woolly hats.

44. A Wesleyan Sunday School procession at Old Bolingbroke, three miles south-west of Spilsby. The village can claim to be the birthplace of King Henry IV in 1366.

45. Queuing for water at Osbournby, six miles south of Sleaford, in February 1909. Children routinely got involved in everyday tasks and were expected to look after siblings. Only 392 people lived in the small village in 1904.

46. Owston Ferry Church School on a postcard from E.L. Scrivens of Doncaster. The local elementary school was a focal point of villages for children under 12. The village is in the Isle of Axholme, where most of the land was reclaimed from the river. Trading in cattle was an important business there a century ago.

47. A church congregation at Pinchbeck in 1906 on a postcard published by Peakome of Boston, posted at Spalding. Sunday School was a regular part of most children's lives.

48. The green outside the village church at Revesby, six miles south-east of Horncastle, where a group of girls on the right is performing 'Ring-a-ring-a-roses'. Postcard published by A. Blades of Horncastle.

49. Children on the river bank at Scopwick on a card by W. Odling of Navenby, posted from the village in August 1913. It is hard to imagine parents letting a group of youngsters roam free like this on such a steep bank today - though it could, of course, have been a specially-arranged photo!

50. The Church Lads Parade at Skegness in August 1918, all perfectly presented in their uniform, including canes. Religious bodies were very important in providing outlets for young people.

51. The Derby and Derbyshire Children's Seaside home in Skegness. All the girls are in their summer dresses and the boys in shorts and all wearing their summer hats. Card published by A. Buchanan & Co. of Thornton Heath, Surrey, and postally used in August 1925.

52. George V's coronation in June 1911 provided an opportunity for communal activities. This street party was organised at Gainsborough and featured on a card published by D. Girdlestone of Spital Terrace, Gainsborough.

53. It would be difficult to find a more animated postcard scene than this. It shows the Cycle Parade on Southgate, Sleaford on August 5th - year unspecified, but possibly 1905. The cycles are in the following group behind the band, there isn't a policeman in sight, and random children, including a girl with a pram, are stealing the band's thunder!

54. A line-up of children at Spridlington, nine miles north-east of Lincoln, on a card sent from Caistor to Lincoln in February 1921. Just 252 people lived here at the start of the 20th century. This looks like the entire roll-call of the village school.

55. Methodist Sunday Schools played a huge role in village life a century ago. This group of children is outside the Spilsby Wesleyan Methodist Church (founded in 1814), seen on a postcard published by F. Bundock of Spilsby.

The Sands, Sutton-on-Sea.

5190.

56. Even the adults enjoy a ride on the donkeys along the sands at Sutton-on-Sea. A lady to the right is dressed in a long, heavy dress, not compatible with the beach, pushing the pram. Edwardians did not take their clothes off on the beach, for reasons of propriety and because a sun-tan had not yet been deemed fashionable. Bathing was conducted from changing huts wheeled into the sea. This card was posted to Eastwood, Nottinghamshire, in September 1905.

Torksey

57. Village children at Torksey, nine miles north-west of Lincoln, featured on a postcard sent to Saxilby in March 1908.

58. The last recorded 'ran-tanning' took place at Washingborough in 1910. The object of this custom (similar to the stocks and ducking stool, and dating back to medieval times) was a local who had been found 'guilty' of wife-beating. The villagers armed themselves with anything that would make a noise, including drums, accordians, buckets, sticks and improvised home-made instruments, and the resultant din was continued day and night outside the 'offender's' house. This 1910 event was possibly a staged revival rather than a genuine ran-tanning. Plenty of children took part in it.

59. Another card from W. Odling of Navenby showing an Edwardian scene at Welbourn, 12 miles south of Lincoln.

60. Bicycles often featured in postcard photos of the Edwardian period. This 1905 scene shows a group of children on Sleaford Road, Wellingore, a village nine miles north-west of Sleaford.

61. The baby show at Willingham Fete in 1912, where both babies and parents are dressed up for the occasion. Card published by Howard Welchman of Gainsborough.

62. Chapel Lane in West Butterwick where the girls are all in their pristine white pinafore dresses. The village is on the River Trent in north Lincolnshire, and a century ago a ferry connected West with East Butterwick.

63. The local hunt meeting outside the village church at Waltham on a cold morning. The arrival of the hunt always proved an exciting spectacle. Girls in the foreground are wrapped up well in their large collared winter coats and hats. Waltham, a small market town four miles south of Grimsby, had its own railway station.

64. An idyllic summer picnic scene at Tetney, six miles south-east of Grimsby, on a postcard sent to Beaconsfield in September 1913.

65. Children have taken over High Street, Owston Ferry, on this postcard published by E.L. Scrivens of Doncaster. As with so many of the postcards featured in this book, the street is empty of wheeled traffic.